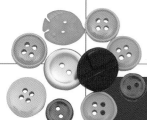

Counting

100 Peanuts

9

2

BY SARA PISTOIA

The Child's World

Published by The Child's World®
1980 Lookout Drive • Mankato, MN 56003-1705
800-599-READ • www.childsworld.com

Acknowledgments
The Child's World®: Mary Berendes, Publishing Director
The Design Lab: Design
Editing: Jody Jensen Shaffer

Photographs ©: David M. Budd Photography

ISBN 9781623235284
LCCN 2013931427

Printed in the United States of America
Mankato, MN
July, 2013
PA02173

ABOUT THE AUTHOR

Sara Pistoia is a retired elementary teacher living in Southern California with her husband and a variety of pets. In authoring this series, she draws on the experience of many years of teaching first and second graders.

Counting

Why do we **count**? Sometimes we want to know how many of something there are. We could guess how many children are in this class. It looks as if there are a few—perhaps seven or eight.

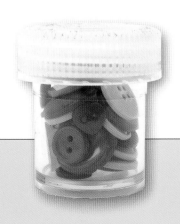

If we want to know exactly how many children there are, we can count them! If there aren't very many things to count, we can count by **ones**.

There are exactly seven children. When there are fewer than ten in a group, it's easy to count by ones.

Look at all the geese! It looks as if there are more than ten. Let's count by **fives** to see how many geese there are.

How many groups of five are there?

Could all of the geese fit into groups of five?

We need to count by fives first. Then we count the rest by ones.

When you count the geese by fives, there are two groups of five. Two groups of five make ten. But there are two more geese! That means there are twelve geese walking in the grass.

How could we count all these buttons? We could count them by ones. But we can count them more quickly if we group them into piles of five.

Count by fives as you point to each pile.

Six piles of five is thirty! Is there a quicker way to count?

Now try counting the buttons by **tens**.

First, group the buttons into piles of ten.

Did you count three piles of ten? Good!

Three piles of ten is thirty.

ones

When you counted by fives, you pointed to six piles. Remember? But when you counted by tens, you pointed to just three piles.

Look at this pile of rocks. What's the best way to count them? If you said by tens, you're right!

First, sort the rocks into groups of ten.

Are there some left over? Let's set those aside and count them last. We'll count them by ones.

Did you count six piles of ten? Good! That's sixty! Then count four extra rocks by ones. That's sixty-four rocks!

How can we write the **amount** using **numerals** instead of words? We'll have to remember which numeral shows how many tens we have. And we'll have to remember which numeral shows how many ones we have.

We write the number of tens on the left. We write the number of ones on the right. Each number has its own **place value**.

tens	ones
6	4

If you write "46," you are saying there are 4 tens and 6 ones. But if you write 64, you are saying there are 6 tens and 4 ones.

Do you like jelly beans?
Which bag would you choose?

If you like jelly beans, you want
the bag that contains more.
Which bag has more?

What if you choose the bag with fourteen (14) jelly beans on the left? You'll get one group of ten plus four more jelly beans.

What if you choose the bag with forty-one (41) jelly beans on the right? You'll get four groups of ten jelly beans, plus one extra!

tens	ones
4	1

If you get both bags of jelly beans, how many do you have? You can add the numbers and find out.

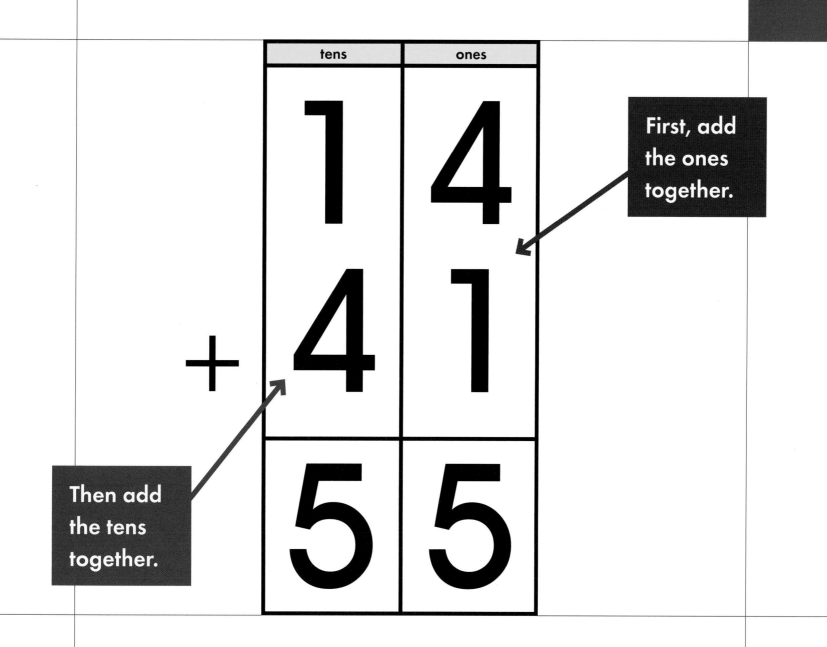

First, add the ones together.

Then add the tens together.

Wow! This bag holds a lot of peanuts!

What if you counted ninety-nine (99) peanuts plus one more? You would need another special number—

one hundred (100)!

To write one hundred, we add a number to the left of the tens. When you count this many things, you really have to keep track!

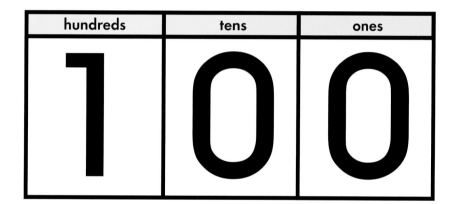

hundreds	tens	ones
1	0	0

Remember to place the numerals in their special places: ones, tens, and **hundreds**.

How many books are there? Count them.

How many kittens are there? Count them.

fives

ones

You can count by ones, by fives, and by tens. And you can keep track of how many things you count. Just be sure to write the numbers in their special places.

tens

hundreds

Key Words

amount

count

fives

hundreds

numerals

ones

place value

tens

Index